It's mine!

By Janine Amos and Annabel Spenceley
Consultant Rachael Underwood

CHERRYTREE BOOKS

A Cherrytree Book

Designed and produced
by A S Publishing

Copyright this edition © Evans Brothers Ltd 2003
by Cherrytree Press Ltd
327 High St
Slough
Berkshire
SL1 1TX

First published in 1999

First published in paperback 2003

British Library Cataloguing in Publication Data

Amos, Janine
  It's mine!. – (Good friends)
  1.Friendship – Pictorial works – Juvenile literature
  I. Title II.Annabel Spenceley
  302.3'4

ISBN 1 84234 154 5

Printed and bound in Malaysia

The treasure map

Everyone is making treasure maps.
There is one piece of gold paper left.

"It's mine!" says Amie.
"I want it!" says Gemma.

5

"We can both use it!" Amie tells her.
Amie starts work at one end of the paper.

Gemma agrees. She works at the other end.

They make the treasure map together.

"It looks great," thinks Gemma.

"It's finished! I'll put it on my bedroom wall," says Amie.

"I want it on my bedroom wall!" says Gemma.
How do you think Gemma feels?

11

"I've got an idea," Steve tells them.
"Would you like to hear it?"

"One of you could take it home today.
The other can take it tomorrow."

"Yes, let's take it in turns!" says Amie.

"Who'll go first?" wonders Gemma.
"You can!" Amie offers.

At hometime, Gemma picks up the map carefully. "Thanks, Amie," she says. "Tomorrow it's your turn!"

16

The tiger mask

Alex comes to play at Callum's.

Callum has made a mask.
It is a tiger mask.

He puts it on.
"Grr!" goes Callum.

Callum strides around the room.
"Grr! Grr!" he growls.

"I want it!" says Alex.
He grabs the mask.

Callum pulls away.
"It's mine!" he shouts.

Alex pulls and Callum pulls.

The mask is broken.

Callum starts to cry.

Callum's mum comes over.
"Oh, it's broken," she says. "What can we do?"

"We can fix it. We can tape it back,"
says Alex.

Callum gets the tape.
Together they fix the mask.

Now Callum is a tiger again.

And Alex is Batman.

"It's mine!" If we want the same thing at the same time as someone else it can be a problem.

We can work it out by talking, sharing, taking turns or finding something different to play with. There are often many ways to solve a problem.